AF433343

SONGS

AND

POEMS

Felice Picano

Copyright© 2020 Felice Picano
ISBN: 978-93-90202-16-4

First Edition: 2020
Rs. 200/-

Cyberwit.net
HIG 45 Kaushambi Kunj, Kalindipuram
Allahabad - 211011 (U.P.) India
http://www.cyberwit.net
Tel: +(91) 9415091004 +(91) (532) 2552257
E-mail: info@cyberwit.net

No part of this book may be reproduced or transmitted in any form or by
any means, electronic, mechanical, photocopying, or otherwise, without
the express written consent of Felice Picano.

Printed at Repro India Limited.

for Stephen Myrick III
who may sing these one day

Contents

1

EARLY SONGS AND POEMS

COUNTRY-POP SONNET

Some folks say rainbows have an end
Where treasure waits for those who dare.
While others say that life's to share
With a fated love, or one true friend.
But I've seen men who waste their lives
Chasing ideals, that I'd call lies.
And I've known men who'll always try
To turn encounters into wives.
. . . Now, I don't want that abstract gold
Somewhere just around the bend.
And I don't want that dream affair
'Cause dreams will pass, and we'll get old.
I'd just like two clear minds to blend
And when I turn, to see you there.

SONG FOR SUSAN

Call up Susan!
She's back from California
Wearing ribbons of despair
In her hair.
She's the Grand Canal of sorrows.
She's forgotten how to care.
She's alone now.

Go see Susan!
How she's changed!
How the "Frisco mist
And a man she can't name
Have drained out all her light.
She's so tight
Just sitting there,
Rapping her cares all around her!

Talk to Susan!
Try to tell her
How it's happened once or twice
To everyone half-nice
Even you,
And her West Coast love affair
Was an adolescent passion —
She won't listen.

Susan! Susan!
She's gotten herself in a love-trap.
All she can see is a road map

Felt tip green lines
Leading eastward,
Leading nowhere.
And she's spent so long in leaving
She can't believe she's made it
Back to here!
Oh, Susan!

And some months later
You're certain to hear
From several strangers and several near
How Susan's going back.
She's already packed.
To try it just once more
Oh! Susan!

ADMIRATION

for R.A.L.

You're so clear
Even the mist knows it.
Look at it hover
And descend all around us:
Weeping eternal slow wetness
Into everything real
That it touches
What a clammy lover
What a devourer of color!
Even the crystal is
Damp food for its hunger.
It defends itself
Only from you.
Lifting aloof, it spirals
In angry blue drops—
Nothing like dew—
On the tips of your hair.
What a halo it makes
Under streetlights!

WAITING ROOM

From the moment I bought it
I thought it was a church pew –
All long and dark wood spare:
I saw it distinctly Lutheran –
Until the day I lay down upon it,
Smoking the butt end of a cigarette
And you said I was the picture
Of a small-town travelling hobo
Passing the night on the bench
Of a railroad station.

Then I knew the idea of a pew
Had brought on a great delusion:
For here, clearly, in my living room
To one side of the fireplace,
Opposite the gate-leg table,
Half reflected in the looking glass —
The bench sits, squat and strong
Transforming it all
from a home to a true waiting room.

And here I will wait. Isn't that
Why I'm redecorating?
Procrastinating? Despite all my plans
For Big Sur, and the South
Of France? Yes. Here I will wait
Until unsated ambitions are filled.
Won't you come and have some tea?
And wait with me?

Wait till your lover has come.
Wait till desires are gone.
Wait until Pluto hits Mars.
Wait, just to wait, in my waiting room?

IS THIS IT, MR. POE?

Man in a crowd
Surrounded by no one
Gets his personal yes
From the overflowing.

Man all alone
Watching the motion
Can't know in advance
Where the tide is going.

So he follows, always follows.
And the sidewalks are
Cardboard stairways to a palace
Always crumbling just
As he gets there. Nothing's
Happening there. Does it
Matter? In your mind's eyes
Isn't life just clatter, just splatter?
Do you follow? Always follow?

Man all alone
You're not eating too well
You've been missing your sleep
And it's showing,

Man in a crowd
Get away from that glass.
It's *my* reflection there
That you're throwing!

APPLES

An apple
Just isn't
A
poem.
It's a red skin spun
'round a seed filled core
with sweet white meat
in between.
Then
again,
it's a tall golden goblet
one side slightly flushed
with shiny pink frankness
from the orbs central stem
to its stub little legs
Or,
it's a mottled green gourdlet
not spongy, all acid in the tip
of your tongue when you
nip at it. Easy for slicing.
perfect for pie. Striped outside
and in.
But
Whatever
its shape
and
however
its taste,
whether you're

calling it
"Delicious"
"Fuji" Red Rome"
"Northern Spy"
It's always
an apple.
never a poem.

Here's three. Have one.

MINIATURES

1.
Cats watching shadows
And jumping plaster walls
To scratch at them—
That's what I like about life:
We're not alone
In the greatest delusions

2.
This world of mine—
How can I best describe it?
A final thrust of dreaming flesh,
A burst of dew,
Then wetness.
After all those complications!

3.
Recognizing infinity
In a swirling mote of coffee
I sat back
And let it take me through …..
These instants add up
. . . Eventually.

4.
A Chinese rocket,
A firefly reverting to air,
A glitter of detail
In an oil by Vermeer,

Gold spider grown leggy,
A sun flare tail:
Thank you for
yellow
chrysanthemums!

HOMAGE TO EMILY D.

Resentment always slithers in
heavily disguised:
It wears the robes of innocence
Woven tight with lies:
Born from unjust incidents
–united by minor size—
It growls each day with discontent
Proofs buzzing the mind like flies.
Suddenly— all peace is lost— in jeopardy
And nightmares fill your eyes.

From ON THE MORTON STREET PIER: A POEM SUITE

1.

I'm sitting on the wooden ledge
At the fartherest edge of the pier.
Ocean liners and sea-trains choked
With prepackaged blue cargo slide by
Doing a relativity trip:
When the hull's lined up parallel
You would swear that the pier
Not the boat, was doing the floating.
Isn't it a sight? Einstein was right!

2.

At lunchtime – noon to two—local
Office workers come here to picnic.
Girls in fours and men in groups
Parade the pier as if on Mars.
They're curious. They giggle,
Grab some sun, then take off.
A few with lunches still in hand
Sit and settle longer to nibble.

Construction crew's guys
Visit and openly tease faced with
men hand-in-hand, face to face.
And sometimes, after work's done,
They come out alone, looking more closely.
Some are curious. Others civil.
Some stroll, then take off.
Others settle to nibble.

3.
Radios blare baseball game innings,
Callas arias and the Beatles' last hit.

Firetrucks whoop siren songs along the West Side
Highway, swooping around bends like slot-cars.

While Helicopter rotors keep
Intercepting naps you try to take.

Across the Hudson where Palisades
rise, is a cool, wooded grove — to city eyes:

A twenty-story tower from a Sci Fi
comic cover, juts from a tenement dock:

Slung low white pleasure boat at shoreline
—sun or smog—is parked every day of the week:

Paint-by-numbers clumps of trees makes it seem
a little bit of Rio, surprisingly close to Hackensack.

4.
On ascertained sunny days
The Quaker House inmates
Come out to play –flotillas
Of wheelchairs and crutches.

Sudden rush-noise-confusion
As children out of nightmare race:
Braces smashing sidewall wood,
Crutches scraping concrete,
Until they finally stumble,
Jerk short of their target and fall.
Then shrieks break hurtling
from misconstrued voice-boxes
like hundreds of gulls gone mad.

They do not frighten, nor repel
These errors of love, unsubtle distortions
of genes' mixing or star's locations.
They run, shout, fall –all of it despite!
Eliciting joy out of motes in the sky.
They exalt the morning.

5.
"Bambi" has slept on the pier all night
My dear, he's really a wreck:
Hair flattened out like a welcome mat,
Clothed in perpetual madness.
He's sunning now, pre-first drink of the day,
Inspecting his dehydration,
Laughing at clocks and the morning.

Enter one retired man (most distinguished)
Carrying a *Times*, a thermos of cocktails,
And folding chair under one arm.
He passes by Bambi and sneers.
He would have drawn the Fool
If he'd done his own Tarot that morning.

Because Bambi jumps up real sudden,
A character actor in a grade-B movie.
Bambi bows, Bambi fawns, Bambi finally shouts
"Good Morning, your highness! Good morning!"

6.
Amsterdam, Rotterdam,
Antwerp, The Hague—
Names from adventure tales
Read as a child;
Cities I've driven through,
Dined in or screwed in:
Now letters stenciled
On ocean liner sides.

It's sudden one morning—
A ship is moored at standstill.
Before was just river and pier.
Three days of stick figures
Wash down cone funnels
Like so many horse-flies –annoying.
Three days of female tones
Announce on the P.A.
Lunch will be served on deck four.

One night: portholes light.
Chatter collides in iced-glasses.
Miss Liberty smiles on her bay.
The next days, it's sailed:
Confetti in spider's webs
Trails through steel girders,
Dangles in rainbowed spots,
Rots in the damp air and spray.

Amsterdam, Rotterdam,
Antwerp, The Hague—
Bicycle cities:
Small, old, provincial.
From where I sit, melting hot
They are towns in adventure books,
Lord how exotic! How far!

REPAINTINGS

1. MYSTICAL MARRIAGE

Symmetry:
A bird at rest
revolves its head to preen
Sassetta's ladies waft in total trinity.
St. Francis always marries
Lady Poverty. His sadness
Is the almost
Of bestowing one slim ring.

Barefoot,
Ever airborne,
The care-torn wife looks back:
Tolls whispering Siena
Through open fresco light.

Then
Earthly ties ignited
Her colors furl regret.,

2. NORFOLK

A visiting poet. A subtle diplomat.
A lover, addicted to beauty. Aristocrat
by stance and the honor of the ducal chain
which never quite defines you.
Northern Apollo nude, hidden in midnight velvet.
Lurker through mists and lagoons. Canal
Dreamer. Reveler in festivals. Witness
To tortures we only can guess at.
Baconian empiricist. Follower
Of the logical Machiavel. Confident
In the power of paint, the legend of Titian
For all time to come: with a hand on your hip
You casually dare me to root out the secret
Locked tight in the lapis centuries
Of your eyes.

3. A SCROLL BY MU CHI

Six persimmons
are
soon to be

eternally
dewsweetjuice
fleshcoolfruit

ripe
to
eat.

4. HILLYARD'S COMPLAYNT TO HIS MODEL: A SONNET

Today these hawthorn buds so fill my sight
That surely they had warning you'd desire
To walk with me within this greenwood briar
And, sensing that I perceive, but by your light,
To show themselves indifferently white:
Their color I'd compare, and find yours higher.
I think that Nature's folk do all conspire
To blind me quite, that you may beam more bright.
For when I frame you in this garden bower
And picture your curled youth like one rich flower
Shadows do invade, remind that petals fade,
That vines do wither, this sunlight dies in shade.
So more must I labor — to stay this mortal hour
Through all my tinting craft, and passions' power.

IN MEMORIAM: WYSTAN HUGH AUDEN, 1973

(1907-1973)

1.
October first:
a supermarket aisle,
myself and an old friend meet
between pre-packaged pie crusts
and dairy foods.

He's a social worker now
and enjoying it.
Two of his boys were accepted at Harvard.
He's fed on their achievements:
prouder than a father.
And what have I been doing?

I begin the three-minute *precis*
everyone carries for such an occasion:
The ups and downs
The hopes deferred
The dreams re-aroused;
The blond down on a pair of thighs
The angle of sun on the Big Sur range:
a life encapsulated—
worse than a lie.

Metal carts keep slinging by.
I'm caught on the tape-end of carrots.

Lots of excuse-me's.
Then he slides into the news
"Well, now that Auden's gone…"
It's the first I'd heard
I question his facts
a little bit shocked.
His tight smile relents,
as though reading a list
—sugar, salt, cream cheese—
he piles on the details
culled from an obit that weekend.
Surely, I had seen it?

Each little fact of death
comes out shiny and clean
wrapped neat as the chopped round
he tosses into the shopping cart last.

How can you hear an era end
in the whoosh of a push-pad
supermarket door?
Whistlings in the rubber grooves,
gravely intoning, "Auden's gone"?

Auden's gone.

2.
Had to work late tonight.
Couldn't make it to the memorial services.
Didn't want to go anyway . . .
A fluttering congregation
all gathered to blather sounds
they hope will come out as Requiems.

Who needs it?
I'll take the subway platform instead.
A shopping-bag lady, boozy and itching.
A black couple necking.
A man refolding his *New York Times*.
The clangor of the E Train doors closing.

They call to mind some attributes:
How he was aloof and pedantic among strangers,
seemed indifferent to issues,
experimental with his trove of ideas,
warm, curious of me—a young man
in a turtle neck sweater, sport coat I'd worn
just to re-meet him, all ardor and beard.
And how kind!

3.
No solemn music
in uptown cathedrals
suffices ....

Ice cubes in glasses clink
chatter goes on
a prelude by Chopin hangs
wrinkling in air
a visitor passes
the anteroom doorway
wreathlets of cigarette smoke
glide by the eyes
the softness of roses
astonish.

And he
who was the uncommon mind
of the common life
and could speak of these
better than you or me—
is not.

4.
The last martini
has been shaken and tasted.

And it's dry.
Very dry now.

2

LATER SONGS AND POEMS

LIFTED

Three men in a boat
on a lake in the Alps
never knew
what it was that hit them—
They were lifted!

Seventeen Taiwanese
Girls at sewing machines
rose as one
like a great tidal wave —
They were lifted!

Two tenors in the choir
Of a Compton A.M.E.
Split a high C –so naturally
everyone else there joined them—
They were lifted!

We are down, we are up
First we're living so mightily
We are up, we are down
Then we're suddenly lost at sea
Holding on by the edge
Oh! our fingers will soon fly free
And we'll fall, yes, we'll fall
Not from sin — but from gravity.

We are up, we are down
Isn't it time to forget TV

And those banks and the boss
Got us wrapped up so tightly
First we're down, then we're up
If you want to— you can be free
Look up there, see the sky
Let yourself be lifted on high

You'll be lifted
We'll be lifted
We'll all be lifted!
Lifted on high! Lifted!

NEW ORLEANS GIRLS

Shape shifting Mamas
on St. Peters Square
tell your Fate for a ten spot
while a coronet wails
and a high-hat whisks warnings
you can almost believe …
whispering all kinds of jazz
about New Orleans girls

New Orleans girls!
Skin smooth as a new-made beignet
New Orleans girls!
Chickory flavor in every caress
New Orleans girls!
Drambuie kisses
and Tupelo honey,
Oh, and it's true they
will spend all your money!
No hurricane's bad as those
New Orleans Girls

Went down to Bourbon
to have me a time.
I've got no woman,
I've got zero ties.
Silken waitress at Brennan's
fed me Oysters Anne Rice.
I stayed on past midnight,
Then we split in a cab. . . .

New Orleans girls!
Confederate flag fingernails!
New Orleans girls!
Bite so soft when they kiss you…

Can't recall what she said
If she told me her name.
Got an itch on my neck
that I cannot explain. …But
I can't stay away. No!
I'm headed back now
for more New Orleans girls.

ASHES AND ICE

We're locked in a room
in a Vegas hotel
Twenty-eighth floor
Emptied out bar
Pizza sauce bleeds
On the penthouse door.
First came here to deal.
First came here to steal
Now we're here to finally
have it all out –You and me.
We were such a great team!
No one could ever touch us!
Ashes and Ice!

Chapel bells once
rang rings round our heads.
Our lives were our own
To be envied.
Then you broke our first rule,
Now I'm flat on the floor
You're out cold on the bed
Which one's the fool?
Ashes and Ice!

Yes, we ran all the games
Trashed each other's good name
Now we're stuck in a burnt room
On the twenty-eighth floor
Photos and CDs scattered around —

And we'll leave here feet first.
Yes, we came here
to finally end it in
Ashes and Ice!

BREAK DOWN

Gliding through sky blue buttes
Ragtop down and fluttering
No better ride for a city dude
'Til my Chevy starts a-stuttering

Swerved to the side
it's a lonesome road:
just succulents and loco weed
Phoned Triple A
when that tow truck arrived
the mechanic was cuter than anything

Sam's the name
I read on her cap.
Tough as bolts
she got under the hood
lots of "hmm,"
lots of muttering,
I fell in love as she
spelled out the news:

—You got a busted carburetor
And your alternator's shot
Those hoses there look ratty
Gas line's downright iffy
Every belt inside needs changing
It's wonder you got this far.

Oh, Sam's the name
I read on her cap.
Samantha it was
when we married.
It's HoneySam when
we're both in bed
And Sammy-Who? When
I'm catting around.

I got a busted carburetor
And my alternator's shot
My extremities are ratty
My arteries are iffy
Every organ I got needs exchanging
—It's a wonder I got this far.

Oh, Sam's the name
I read on her cap.
Samantha it was
when we married.
It was Watch-Out-Sam!
when we hit the skids
and Sammy-So Long
when she left me for dead.

SONNET

Linger warm, September shadows
Autumn's come this year so bold
glints of winter trace my windows
wings are frosted, leaves laced cold.
All things natural fall in slumber
all succumb but –I protest!
Spring was far too sudden a wonder
here an instant, then passed on West.
I beg you, send a hot November.
Birds and insects still will migrate.
Mammals still store food and sleep late.
I'll bask in a Bermuda pretender
'till Summer illusions are icily humbled
and the locks of time summarily tumbled.

MOTET

Not because it is the center midpoint heart
but because threads converge:
man-stuff music-stuff:
notes hang on spiderwebs
crystals discover hidden matrices
protein carries floorplans into life.

That is why song occurs.
The welling-up, thorax in release,
breath taken in, the white zone
in the head.

            And all about
vibrations foliate branches:
twigs: the weave of a desk's impan-
-elling, the extension of a sleeve.

When we bend metal –I Beam or
paperclip –within begins
a process that might not ever end.
Who is to say steel cannot sing
a *laudamus*, that a trill
does not determine a universe?

BIRTH MARKS

We are pleased and thrilled with human imperfection
The mask from within that flaps a dewlap distortion
not seen on anatomical charts: the girl with oak-tree hair,
the man with a cobra penis. We are all amazed
and delighted to discover. But listen, all
of us carry our mark, as though genes burst at birth
to leave a signature, to say this is individual: new:
accomplished— despite the rules –once more.

Mine is a two-inch spatter of rash on my left arm bicep.
Over the decades I've learned to perceive it as proof,
when young of desired Cherokee blood. Later, as a swan in flight,
the ugly duckling gone. It's clear and bold, seldom hidden
brown when I'm tan, angry when I'm pale. I kiss it for luck,
touch it in private when I pass some more obvious monster,
reiterate my claim to being, to uniqueness.

Odd that friends seldom see it, that lovers discover it
only some months later, that my mother touched it once
and asked if I'd been burnt. She who bathed that very spot
from infancy. Yes, I told her: burnt into life.

HIS SECRET

(after learning of R.F.'s diagnosis)

Questions are etched on the winter garden's glass.
How should one respond to what's already
Been long known? How far, really, should one go?

Everyone has fair reason to reveal —-or to hold.
Still, fear lies thick amid the flatware of Tea's
civility, outlasts games of Patience on the porch.

But what to say when the phone rings … just so?
Accommodation has so many drawbacks.
Couldn't one simply . . . get it over?

.. And the mantle of once more being selected
For an unwanted secret clutches
the shrugged shoulders of the "unaffected."

Once more, favors will be repaid in triplicate
As, inversely, time passed in his company
trebles in value … and in complications.

For exactly how long, and in which situations
—being poured out or played out (quietly trumped)—
are you and I already little but memory?

A LATE AUBADE

It is that moment of stillness
When wet sheets are hung to dry.
The afternoon storm we ignored
Has fled back to the ocean:
tiny lightnings attempt
to frighten by distant striking.
Rainwater dribbles onto
deck wood crumbling outside.
It's sound is so soft
we are made drowsy with consistency.

Tableaux are reconstructed
every time our bodies budge.
Bedclothes furl as though
for a camera's cool vision.
Fingers strum upon skin
half-forgotten toccatas,
our heads so close
hair meshes, lips brush as we speak
faces become geologies.

It is the hour of a hot pink dusk
which will never be unveiled
of torpor after making love:
of delight in once more taking
each other by surprise.
Yet omen hangs like a dare
with a vague and stagey warning.
Your eyes close and you sleep.
I slide over your breast
and sip musk from your armpit.

MY MOTHER'S LIFE

This tiny, kitsch-constructed kitchen
Connotes a sober final coda
To the decades-long row of Sunday lunches
She has cooked and I have eaten.
Her life doled out in dinners,
lunches, breakfasts. Her place
and station fixed –not by the occasional
glamour of cocktail furs
the polished power of V-8 sedans
or vacation mountain sunsets—
but by cherished rites in kitchens:
the breakfast nooks I sat in
nibbling my way through adolescence
that she presided over, sad as a Madonna
riven with divorce, or eager as coed
to hear of tax-investment tips. Pensive,
laughing, expansive, annoyed,
in command always in her kitchen.

This is the smallest I have seen
Her heir to, yet she fits it
To perfection. For she has gotten
Smaller too: weight down, inches chipped
From her height as the children shot up,
Become gray haired, then white.
It is spotless, of course, well designed.
The cinnamon range is professional,
all-electric. The ovens equal to any

recipe. The double door icebox taller than I
am glitters like a monument.

Upon one shelf a ceramic duck
Opens its back to quivers of colored
Toothpicks. I cannot imagine
a universe without this object's exis
-tence. Miniscule, unattractive,
accessory, it stands –and every crisis
Comes out right. So, although the flatware
That clinks in our dishes is unfamiliar,
The china finer than any I'd used
Still— an old sugar bowl's glass
Tickles my thumb with its cut,
unperilous edges, and I might be eight years
old again. She shakes the table drawer
that holds the spoon she threatens us
with if we don't eat up: and all of it.

She knows this will be her last kitchen.
Apology floats in her gestures.
She is aware it hasn't the mahogany'
magnificence of the pre-menopausal
glory, not even the charm––surrounded
by lawns, by maples in fire––of
her second marriage. And, as I arrive,
she sits me down, feeds me soup, relates
a dream she's recently had. Fills me with dread
her tastiest broth cannot disguise, Within
her words, like a bone to the throat,
is an omen of death –a death she fears,
hopes for, embarrassed, reveals
commenting how strange she sometimes feels.

This lunch, then, is our last together.
And it is fitting to have heard it here.
Not in the green little living room,
Not in the pink papered sewing room,
but here, where she slides over a plate
insisting I take just one more bite
absorb what must be, chew it to bits,
while she serves up her fate. With style
and concern —a hostess in her own kitchen.

JUNE 26, 2015

Had he lived
would we be celebrating
our momentous today?
Or quietly, simply, be letting it go
having had it, lived it
for ourselves so long?
Not ever requiring
The officious
official
authentication?

Could the sidewalk
revelers we do not stop
to relish, recall
that evening's evening star
kiss a crescent moon,
and splashily silver the piazza:
the Chilean pianist's final,
near-silent, pianissimo —
in c minor: astonished
to hear our wild applause
….so deep in meditation.

Had he lived
would palm and frond and fern and cedar
still be spiny pine and elder alder
rimed icy tight?
And night's aromas not be
Hollywood honeysuckle soft

but copper nasal hot
like sunsets on the Hudson
that still stupefy and hurt
with chemical orange?

Had he lived
would his photo-face be replaced
by one far less familiar
than that insufficiently frequent,
five a.m. r.e.m image. . . .
that makes me wake in wonder
and feel blessed all day long?
No mirage I swear
but across that Wild Divide ....
another kind of communication?
—Had he lived?

WINDOW ELEGIES

1. THE PHOTO IN THE WAREHOUSE

My idea was Manichean—light versus dark
Apexes and triangles intrigued me
I sought a statement of textures, planes
juggled, volumes sounded, a contrasted repose.
my problem –scarcely formalized—was formal,
compositional, mere craft.

The camera was new, hardly used,
a gift from a sister who'd spoken so fast
instructions were mostly a blur,
I just a fiddler with lenses and speeds.
But I knew what I thought, knew what I wanted,
wanted what I saw that day to endure.

Wanted you, for example, the happenstance
model. How to speak of us without exaggeration
is easy. How to convey too little more fraught.
Consider perhaps a parabolic affair,
Neither in rise, nor descending,
Caught featherlike, spinning, mid-air.

Our shared times flash by: an unwritten
novel: the fated encounter at dockside,
your dog's dark, sweet muzzle, nuzzling my lap,
afternoons midweek entangled in sheets,

your taste –part urine, part anisette,
strobes strafing your biceps: palomino, blue, blood.

The warehouse by the Hudson is gone now.
The doorway you stood in torn down for some
multi-laned highway to come. Deceptive warm
Shadows mix like cloth on the floorboards.
corrugations of walls glint unarmed as chrome butter.
Accurate. Tactful. Your silence. My wishes. What was….

I was sick to my stomach the day of those photos.
A Flu for a week. I'd sit up, dress, laugh
then churn whiter than yogurt.
Cramps snaked my intestines with ragged glass
fingers. I fell off the toilet. Cried out
for my mother. Seconds later felt better.

You called by to cheer me. Photos were shown,
the Nikon brought forth. Expeditions suggested.
The warehouse attracted: we'd been there
before and liked the space—stretching.
When we came on that doorway, I knew
we had found it. Fine-eyed always, you chose it.

Saw then what I would only discover later:
how it framed you, how the swirling metal
swept open a Venetian opera curtain.
how sunlight spanned yellow October on the river,
chipped glass transformed to Topaz beneath your heels.
Penumbral within, I placed you and focused

As though I could help it. Asked you to pose
asked you to expose me. I'd gone without breakfast,
I'd eat beauty instead. I said loosen the pants
now drop them. Face away. Better. Sun burns
red through one palm, gilds the globe of a buttock,
a Georges De La Tour with our star for a candle.

You were born to be a cameraman's lover.
In another, less vulgar era, you'd be
a Vatican politician's pampered amore,
a Peloponnesian water-boy lover.
Our times are bereft of the art of companions.
Only you break the mold. Early on you had learned

To accept your self-absorption, had nibbled
on devotion and kept yourself slim. You knew
when to win, sensed the mercy in withholding,
lived out mystery and mischief, knew just when
to give in. It almost seemed unconscious.
This doorway that didn't hold a shred of glass
became a window we once stepped through
in a photo's flash. Our exchange of masks
in timelessness, in affection, for what couldn't
last —a future lost —memories. Others may call
it reality. But all I know are its reflections.

2. THE LOFT

We stood in a row of matched windows
each one spangled with the dark,
coordinated as though in a De Chirico
portico through which a draped
and fleeing figure weaves
her moon splintering night.

This was your airy world, this nest
of little warmth, great heat,
this tower without a turret
easily arrived at by the casket
elevator you warned me
must never be closed.

From these sixteen windows
you looked down, designing patterns
in cobblestones invisible
to those on the ground:
The rhomboid parking lot's
encroachment by brownstone
angles: symbols I never understood.

A world I tried to share, street
level low, in rare conjunctions.
There: the bar we danced in once,
bodies buried within its walls.
here: the concrete perilous
parklet you ran in, Norman

Rockwell updated: boy
in leather jeans, with dog.

This stoa of regular fenestrations
contained a flaw. You revealed
where the carpenters in desperation
had built a ledge to bevel up
illusion. I thought that was a sign
to me. I chose to gloss it over.

Behind us, yards of loft. Domesticated
jungle in one corner. Dolly bed
to roll away –the cow run away with the spoon
—its covers perpetually furled
as though sheets were wrinkled banners,
flags of your utter conquest of me.

Taxi cabs like yellow jackets
sped below. I asked if you checked out
truckers –delivery men delivering men.
You told me no, they were always too far.
instead you said you stood here for hours
staring west at pollution-hued sunsets.

But it was you—you were always too far,
you would frown at the hint of a memory,
cease in mid-sentence, retreat
into traps in your thoughts. Hold
expectation like an overfilled bowl
of hot water, neither you—nor I—dared
look into. We did everything. Did it once.

Passing your building, I sometimes
look up. The sun is too strong, the angle
all wrong — and I see you. You are standing,
shirtless, slender, silent, alone—
waiting like Rapunzel ever self-betrayed
or waiting to enchant my life again,
Or just waiting for the world to come get you.

3. IN THE MUSEUM GARDEN

Ice cracks every atom of our leatherjackets.
Giant granite ladies far too plumply unclad
primp across the unraked gravel. Our flimsy
chairs tilt and softly sway, slightly out of synch.
We are alone again, after three hours of people
—living and avoided, threaded through; or greatly
dead, their artifact souls impaneled for us
to try ourselves before. A late December afternoon
is on display.

       Windows surround us on three sides,
Four, if you count the sheer glass behind the stone
wall we sit in front of: a curtain that will never rise.
No more scenes will follow. Kertesz would have
photographed us here. From on high, perhaps, picking
out five bare trees, little storms of paper
Twirling, two bundled seated men, not talking.

We are though, words the wind slaps across our faces
honing scarves to razor edges. Our voices are low
concrete cold. We could be plotting a hold-up
or government's overthrow. Over one point so often
before in our separate thoughts we're both embarrassed
a little bored. Each freshly said phrase comes out
prearranged.

       I count forty-eight windows.
People can be seen if we shade our eyes from the frozen
light that blanks first this then that glass expanse.

Women in knitted caps, coats dangling; ringed moons
above decaying landscapes. Men checking their watches.
Dali's driven, ever-falling crucifixion.

You are a new you: uncertain yet unpleading. This
showdown hurts, A spot of red has already bruised
your right temple. I would lick it white. But
that would mean surrender. Even so you are more
beautiful than ever, now that I've chosen to lose you.,

When we rise from our seat my ungloved finger
brushes your cheek. We will pull apart soon
and—like a tongue upon sub-zero steel—we will bleed
for years. Windows around us shatter with sun
like flash bulbs exploding as a Rock Star descends
or a madman with a machine gun, as he first opens fire.

4. THE OBLIGATORY SCENE IN A RESTAURANT

We are sitting in a restaurant window
Having lunch again, As though nothing
ever happened. It is two months now.
We are ordering from our menus, playing
with our napkins, taking sips from glasses.
As though it were quite common, we the oldest
buddies, having lunch again.

I am looking at the sidewalk outside
undulate. Couples pass. You complain
about the waiter's camping. We are being
quite adult. As though nothing ever
happened. We talk of this, then that,
him then her. The mustard is too thick,
your beef is far too tough. I haven't got a clue
of what you're seeing, seeing me again.

But what's the sense in asking? We are being
quite adult. So grown up. Showing everyone
Look! We're friends again. After all that.

You are struggling to cut your roast beef,
twelve years old with your embarrassment.
I suggest you ask for a sharper knife.
No. It's okay, you say, and struggle on.
We talk of this, then that, him then her.
two people pass, then come back again
I know I'll never love again, like I did then

With you. Silence re-descends. The waiter brings
a steak knife to our table, unbidden. You take it,
check the fake bone haft, and then hesitate.
Take it, I say, it will be easier: let the
Serrated edge do its butchery. This time
Let's make the cut we make really clean.

ENVOI

It is not precisely as a whisper falls
Seducing the dim air, there, where the inlet
Pretends to be morning; no, nor the soft calls
Of coins as they glitter in a goblet
You let smash. It lives quiet between the bright
And the black, teasing your grasp, misted
Like a mirror a dying man's spite
Makes sigh, an imprint that barely existed.
It is not an obvious loss, as though each day's lining
Were unwound, each hair strung on a thread
Blemish unfound, cache discovered in dread.
No. It is an address vanished, a name past divining
A costlier pain than you ever thought to possess:
Aeons could not explain its sharp hold, its caress.

ACKNOWEDGEMENTS

Many of these poems have been previously published in: *The Connecticut Poetry Review, Cumberland Poetry Review, James White Review, Christopher Street, No Apologies, Kindred Spirit, Chiron Review, Van Gogh's Ear*, in newspapers and in many anthologies. *Window Elegies* was published as a chapbook by the Close-Grip Press at the University of Alabama.